WELLINGTON SQU

GW01185054

When I grow up

John and Marilyn Talbot

Illustrated by Avril Turner

Nelson

Contents

Chapter 1 What do you want to be?

'Today I want you to think about what you want to be when you grow up,' Mr Belter said to the class. 'Think what you want to be ten years from now.'

Lots of hands went up.
Mr Belter asked Rocky first.
'I want to be a fireman,' said Rocky, 'like Fireman Salter.'
'That's good,' said Mr Belter.
'Tell us all about being a fireman.'
'I think it would be very exciting,' said Rocky.
Mr Belter smiled. 'Tell us what you think it would be like to be a fireman.'

'Well,' said Rocky, 'people telephone the fire station for lots of things. They say, "Help! My house is on fire!" or "My cat is stuck up a tree!" or "Come quickly, someone is going to fall off the roof and get hurt!"

'So, I would have to put on my helmet, get in the fire engine and race off with the other firemen.
When we got there we might have to kick in the door to rescue people from a fire, or be brave and climb up a high ladder and get the cat from the tree.

'Sometimes we would have to get out a big net if someone was in danger of falling off the roof.
We would catch them in the net and stop them from getting hurt.
Or I might have to cut people out of a car crash, or put out a bonfire!
As I said, all very exciting!'

'That's very good, Rocky,' said Mr Belter.
Then he asked Ben.

'I want to drive an ambulance,' said Ben.
'Good, Ben,' said Mr Belter. 'Can you tell the
class what you would have to do?'

'Lots of different stuff every day,' said Ben.
'When anyone telephones for an ambulance they say,
"Help, there's been an accident and a lady is hurt!"
or "A boy has fallen into the water and he can't
swim!" or, "Come quickly! A man has banged his
head and he is bleeding!"
I would have to get in the ambulance and race off to
the accident.
We have to get the lady out of the car very carefully,
or rescue the boy who might have drowned, or help
the man who banged his head.
I would have to put them on a stretcher and put them
in the ambulance.
Then I would drive them to the hospital.'

'That's very good, Ben,' said Mr Belter.
'That would be a very important job.'
Then he asked Jamila.
'I want to be a doctor when I grow up,' said Jamila.
'That's good,' said Mr Belter. ' Can you tell us what a doctor does?'

'Well,' said Jamila, 'first of all there is the family doctor. You go and see her when you don't feel very well, and she makes you feel better.
Then, there is the hospital doctor. That's what I want to be. I want to take care of people who come to hospital by ambulance.
It takes many years of training to be doctor and it is really hard work. I think doctors work long hours as well. But I really want to be a doctor and help people who are ill, so I don't mind about that.'

'That's very good, Jamila,' said Mr Belter.
Then he asked Tony.
'I want to be a policeman, like PC Kent,' said Tony.
'Good,' said Mr Belter, 'will you tell us what a policeman does, and why you want to be one?'

'A policeman does lots of things,' said Tony.

'I want to be a policeman because every day would be full of excitement.

People might telephone the police and say, "Come quickly! There is a burglar in my house!" I would get into my police car, put the siren on and race off to help them. I would chase the burglar and catch him red-handed!

Or a little boy might go missing and I would go out and look for him. When I found him, I would take him back to his Mum and Dad.

The police also help out when a bomb is being defused. So, being a policeman can be quite dangerous sometimes.

I think it would be a great job and I really hope I will be a policeman when I leave school.'

8

'Thanks, Tony,' said Mr Belter.
Then he asked Tessa.
'What about you Tessa. What do you want to be?'
'I want to be a reporter,' said Tessa.
'Good,' said Mr Belter. 'What does a reporter do?'

'Well,' said Tessa, 'a reporter can work for radio or television, or a newspaper.
A reporter gets sent to report on lots of different things.
If I was a reporter I might have to write a report on a car accident.
Or I might go to a football match and report on the game.
I would write about who had won the game and who had lost. I would also try and talk to the players, and ask them about the game.
I would have a camera with me, so I could take pictures of the players.

'A reporter often talks to famous people. I might have to talk to someone like Ramona Rome.
I would ask her all about Spot, her pet leopard.
I would ask her if she had any other wild animals at home.

'Sometimes I might have to grab my camera, get in a car and drive to a train crash.
I would have to talk to anyone who saw what happened, and take pictures.
Then my report would be in the newspaper the next day.

'I think it would be really great to be a reporter for a newspaper,' said Tessa,
'and a bit dangerous.'
'Very good Tessa,' said Mr Belter.
'You have tried really hard. Well done!'

Then he asked Kevin.
'What about you Kevin? Tell us what you would like to be.'
But Kevin didn't say what he wanted to be.
Kevin didn't say anything.
He was having a day dream!

Chapter 2 Kevin's day dream

In ten years' time I will have lots of money and I will buy a brilliant car. A sports car!

I will be famous. Lots of reporters will want to take a picture of me.

'Look!' they will say, 'here he comes. That's Kevin Miller.'

I will also be on television.

'One last thing, Mr Miller,' the television man will say, 'what's your favourite colour?'

'Red,' I will say, 'like my sports car!'

Then one day I'll get a letter from my old school.

Waterloo School

Dear Kevin,

You may not remember me but I was your old
teacher before you were famous.
Would you be able to come to Waterloo School for
a day to see your old school?
We would be so pleased if you could find the time
to come back and tell us of your good fortune.

Your old teacher,

Mr Belter.

So, I telephone Mr Belter and tell him, 'Sure, I'll come.'
I drive up to good old Wellington Square.
It's funny seeing the old houses again.
They look so small now.

'We are so pleased and excited to have with us today one of our old boys from Waterloo School,' says Mrs Jones.
'It's Kevin Miller!'
Everyone in the school is standing up.
They all cheer and shout when they see me.
Some of the children start shouting: 'Kevin, Kevin, Kevin...'

'Thank you, thank you, thank you,' I say, but it's difficult to hear. Everyone is making such a lot of noise.

13

I start to speak.
'Ten years ago I was here in this school.
Now look at me!'
All the children are starting to cheer again.
'So remember,' I say, 'one day you can make it to the top like I have. Yes, and you can make lots of money like me. You can become really famous like me!'

'Thank you. Thank you again Mr Miller,'
says Mrs Jones.

Then I go in to see my old class.
Nothing has changed.
Everything looks just the same as it always was.
But Mr Belter looks so old!
I feel sorry for him so I give him fifty pounds.
'Oh, thank you Mr Miller. Thank you!' he says.

There is Jamila.
'Do you still want to be a doctor?' I ask.
'Yes,' she says, 'but it is difficult because there is so much to learn.'
'Keep at it, girl,' I tell her. 'You'll make a good doctor one day.'

Then I see my old friend, Rocky.
'Do you still want to be a fireman?' I ask.
'Yes, I do,' he says. 'But it is difficult, because I get
scared when I am high up on the ladder.'
'You keep at it Rocky,' I tell him, 'because one day
you're going to be a great fireman.'
'Do you really think so, Mr Miller?' he asks.
'You bet,' I say.

Then I see Tony.
'Are you still trying to be a policeman?' I ask.
'Yes I am,' he says, 'but it's difficult because I don't like the sound of the siren.'
'Never mind about that,' I tell him, 'you're going to be a great policeman one day.'
'Do you mean it, Kevin?' he asks.
'Yes, I do,' I say. 'I really mean it!'

Then I see my friend, Ben.
'Do you still want to drive an ambulance?' I ask.
'Yes, I do,' he says. 'But it is so difficult because I can't drive yet!'
'Don't give it another thought,' I say.
'You are going to be a brilliant ambulance man one day.'
'Do you really think so?' Ben asks.
'Yes, I do,' I say.

Then I see Tessa.
'Are you still trying to be a reporter?' I ask.
'Yes, Kevin,' she says, 'but it is so difficult because
I am not very good at talking to famous people.'
'You're talking to me!' I say. 'Tessa, you are going to
be a great reporter one day, believe me.'
'You're not just saying that, are you?' she says.
'No, it's true,' I say.
'Well, can I ask you something?' she asks.
'Sure.'
'Kevin, what do you do for a living?'

'Oh, I'm famous,' I say.
'Yes, but what do you do?' she asks.
'I've got lots of money,' I say.
'Yes, but what do you do?'
'You see that red car over there?'
I am pointing out of the window.
'That's my car!' I say.
'Yes, but what is it that you do?' she asks. 'How did you get your money? Why are you famous? Where did you get that car from?'
Everyone is looking at me.

I can't think what to say.
I have to get away.
'Sorry, Mr Belter, I have to go!'

Chapter 3 Accident!

I run down to my car and drive away as quickly as
I can.
I have to get away from all those people.
I come to some crossroads.
I don't stop.
I go right over.
BANG!
There is a terrible crash.
I hit another car.
Suddenly everything has gone wrong.
For a while I don't know where I am.

'Don't move,' I hear someone say. 'We'll soon get you out of there. I'm a fireman.'
I look up. It's Rocky!
He's a man now.
Rocky and his men are cutting me out of the car.
Then I'm being put on a stretcher and put in an ambulance. I'm being taken to hospital.
'One, two, three, lift!' says the ambulance man.
I look up. It's Ben!
He's a big man now.

Then I get to the hospital.
'Can you move your legs?' asks the doctor.
When I look up, I see that Jamila is the doctor.
Next, a policeman comes in to see me.
He is telling me what happened.
'You didn't stop at the crossroads,' he says. 'You
were going too quickly!'
I look up.
Oh no! It's Tony.
He is also a man now.

I am not badly hurt and soon I can leave hospital.
Someone comes up to speak to me.
'How do you feel after your accident?' she asks.
I look up.
It's Tessa. She's a reporter now.

They are all here. All my friends.
They are calling me.
They want to know how I am.
Kevin...Kevin...
Kevin...

Chapter 4 Crossroads

'Well Kevin, what do you want to be?'
Mr Belter was asking Kevin again.
Kevin woke from his day dream.
The rest of the class was looking at him.
He jumped up.
'I want to be famous,' he shouted out.
Everyone in the room began to laugh.
They laughed and laughed.
Kevin went red.
He felt stupid.

'OK, that's enough laughing,' said Mr Belter.
When the class was quiet he started to tell them
about himself.

'You know I didn't always want to be a teacher,'
he said.
'Like Kevin, I also wanted to be famous and have lots
of money.
When I was a young kid I bought a guitar. Well, the
truth is, I got my Mum and Dad to buy one for me.
Soon, I got together with three other boys. We started
to make our own music.'

'"What name shall we have?" I asked the others.
We thought 'Crossroads' sounded good.
We played our music really loudly.
My Dad would come up and tell me to keep the
noise down.
Word soon got round, and one day we were asked to
play at an end of term party at our school.

Someone made a poster.
"Come to the end of term party!
See Crossroads!"

'We got our stuff ready in the hall.
When the curtains went up we looked great.
We all had the same clothes on: a red coat and
jeans.
When we started to play we sounded brilliant.
Everyone was shouting for more.

Chapter 5 Who wants to be a teacher?

'After the show, a man came up to us and asked if we would like to make a record.
We said that would be brilliant.
He told us to give him five pounds and then he would do the rest to make us famous.
Five pounds was a lot of money back then.
It was hard, but we got the money together and gave it to the man.
Then we waited and waited for him to come back.
We wanted to have a hit record.
We talked excitedly together about what we would do when we were famous.

'But the man who took our five pounds never came back, so Crossroads soon came to the end of the line.
My friends soon went off and did other things.
I didn't know what I wanted to be after that.
In the end, I thought what I really liked doing was helping people.
Then, one day somebody said to me, "What about being a teacher?"
I thought, "That's a good idea. I can help people that way."
So I trained to be a teacher.'

When Mr Belter finished everyone wanted to ask him something.
'Do you like being a teacher?' asked Tessa.

'Well sometimes it's difficult,' said Mr Belter.
'One kid won't talk, and another won't stop talking.
Sometimes it's sad when one of the children has bad news.
Sometimes it's exciting, like on Sports Day or on a school trip.
Sometimes it's funny, like doing the school play.
Sometimes it's frightening.'

'Frightening?' asked Tony. 'Why is it frightening?'
'It can be a little frightening on Open Day when your Mum and Dad come to see me.
There is always someone who is difficult, but usually they are friendly.
So, yes, I do like being a teacher very much,' said Mr Belter.

Mr Belter looked round the class and asked, 'Would any of you like to be a teacher?'
One hand went up really quickly.
It was Kevin.
Mr Belter smiled.
'Good lad,' he said.